Ghost Trawler

Mícheál Fanning

SOMERVILLE PRESS

Somerville Press,
Dromore, Bantry,
Co. Cork,
Ireland

© text Mícheál Fanning

Designed by Jane Stark
seamistgraphics@gmail.com

Typeset in Adobe Garamond

ISBN: 978 0 9562231 28

Printed in Spain

For Nóirín, wonderful wife and mother, Peadar, Ruth and Rachel.
For my family and friends.
We remember my mother, Molly.
We also remember Brendan Sheehan and Bairbre Lonergan
who passed on to The Great Beyond during 2010.

"Works of Art are of an infinite loneliness…
only love can grasp and hold and be just towards them"
From *Letters to a Young Poet* by Rainer Maria Rilke
(translated by M.D. Herter Norton)
Published by W.W. Norton and Company Ltd.

"How much suffering there is to get through"
after Rilke

This publication is a collaboration between artists and the poet. Claire Curneen, Tralee and Cardiff, has offered the cover illustration, IZNIK, and six pieces. There are six other art pieces – one by Fiona Morgan, two by Pat McGrath, Cabra, one by Liam O'Neill, Baile'n Fhirtéaraigh, one by Adrienne Heslin, Ballyferriter, and one by Mick Davis, Baile'n Fhirtéaraigh.

Pictures in *Ghost Trawler*

Book Cover – Iznik (Claire Curneen)
Page 6 – Madonna and Child (Fiona Morgan)
Page 8 – Children . . . Sandy (Claire Curneen)
Page 13 – Blue Angel (Claire Curneen)
Page 18 – Tears and Compassion (Claire Curneen)
Page 20 – Cowboy is Surrounded (Pat McGrath)
Page 22 – An Rás Mór (Liam O'Neill)
Page 24 – Pádraic on Márthain (Adrienne Heslin)
Page 28 – The Mexican (Pat McGrath)
Page 32 – Mary Magdalene (Claire Curneen)
Page 40 – Diogenes (Mick Davis)
Page 43 – House on Shoulder (Claire Curneen)
Page 44 – Figure with Branches (Claire Curneen)

Thanks to P Ó Fionnáin for French translation (page 7)

www.michealfanning.com

Contents

1	The Son praises The Madonna, His Mother	7
2	Children play	9
3	Boy on the Bicycle	10
4	The Blue Train	12
5	Cloud	15
6	Fog	16
7	Beautiful World	19
8	Fenit Pier	21
9	Ráiseanna na mBád 2009	23
10	Ghost Trawler	25
11	Manuela Riedo R.I.P.	26
12	Have we not realized?	27
13	Cocaine	29
14	The Radiant World / An Domhan Gleoite	30
15	Mary Magdalene, only Time will tell	33
16	Thomas Hardy I	34
	Thomas Hardy II – Thomas and Emma Hardy	36
	Thomas Hardy III – Bath	37
	Thomas Hardy IV – Wessex	38
	Thomas Hardy V – Troy	39
	Thomas Hardy VI – Virginia Woolf	39
	Thomas Hardy VII – Death	41
17	St. Molaga, pray for us	42
18	We are all Haitians	45

The Son praises The Madonna, His Mother

(Book of Kells, Folio 7v)

For Nóirín

Maria,
Maria,
Maria.

Mater sanctifica,
"Totus tuus
sum, Maria."

The brightest angels circumornate Her
and The Omniscient is cuddled
in The Hodegetria's bosom.
Hail Nóirín in this beautiful world.
You shine on the bay.
Glory to you on this radiant day.

Na haingil is gile ina timpeall,
is an tEagnaí ina shuí
i mbaclainn an Treoraí,
Dia dhuit, a Nóirín. Glóir do Nóirín sna harda
Glóir duit ar an lá is áille.

Les plus lumineuses anges La circumdécorent
Et l'Omniscient s'abrite
Dans la poitrine de l'Hodegetria.
Je vous salue Noirín dans ce beau monde.
Vous brillez sur la baie,
Gloire a vous ce jour de Mai.

Maria, Maria, Maria.

Children play

The sun shines. The children will play.
Children run over rusty fields of hay
and race into the aquamarine sea.

A woman in an orange swim suit
dives between the waves
 and the spray.

Children play on the eternal shoreline – building
sand castles with green buckets and shovels, another two
children in red Tshirts measure strings of sea-weed

and a child in a navy vest splashes in the sea.
The children swim free on this hazy autumnal day
 across an azure Ballyheigue bay.

for Kay and Philip, Caoilte and Rua

Boy on the Bicycle

Stopping gently secured at the traffic-lights,
my bicycle comes to a soft halt,
I am a ten year-old schoolboy dressed
in my black coat, for comfort in the night.

I pedal on. I turn my head
to remark the people who appear
out of houses. All is quiet in the town
that I love. Night falls.

I freewheel past the homes
of my contented friends, with whom
I cycled round the narrow roads
'round our homes today.

I realize the simple beauty of the evening.
All the people and I
are one in one, as evening turns
with purpose to night.

There is sleep in my heart now. Pushing on
I reach home in high cheer.
Sleep I shall, shall I sleep
        I shall sleep

for there are cushions from heaven
for me to sleep upon
in the golden room, that You, My Father,
the Supreme Artist,

in Your most concerned hour
have fashioned for me,
a room as gentle
and as good.

I sleep into our night,
so that I may recall – girls and
boys pedal on bicycles
        now and forever.

        – Lullaby

The Blue Train

For Lia, Annie and Celia

Finally, comes the time
of day, to me a child,
after many, long, tense
      days

I sleep now, to travel in the blue train
that travels to planet 120 from planet 38.
May I always journey there if I need to
for I own my 5-penny fare.

There are many with fear like mine
on our train, that takes 87 hours
to reach here at its ease. Oh shall you
hear the choir of children from carriage 23

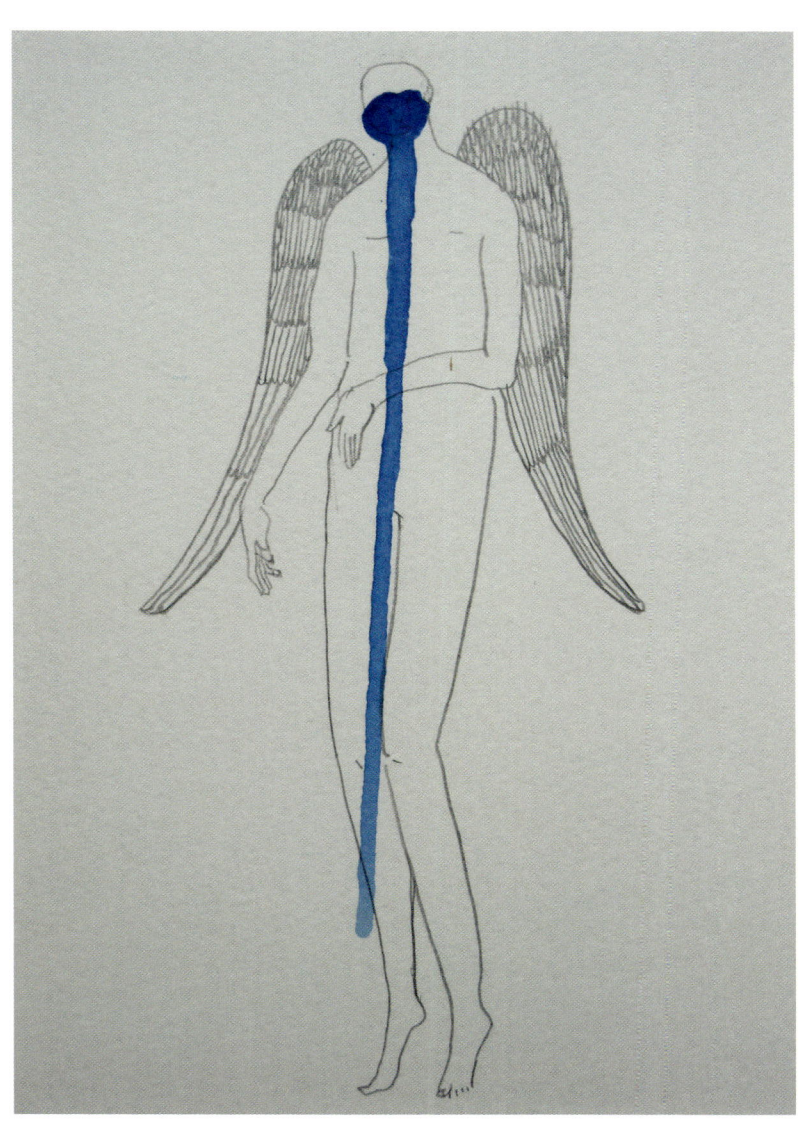

they sing songs that'll always bring tears
to us 300 uncertain children
from our various homes
going to where we don't know where?

The train wends on and on
through the heavens
on through a 100 universes.
Oh there is so much time

to wander on,
laugh and not care
and enjoy the great journey
of three and a half days.

You, our friend, the sky-blue angel,
 whispers – sleep, sleep, my tired children
for there is peace here for each of
you, near the moons somewhere.

– Lullaby

Cloud

I am a cloud sliding along. I am free to live
and love and dance and move with the wind.
I am alive today, not yesterday, not tomorrow.
I am alive now, the suffering is almost over.

O, my story is almost happy, but I was as unhappy
once upon a time.
But I am experienced to deal with the wind, the sun, and
the ice-cold. I serve nature now.

Here I go again, I am free and easy,
joyful and merciful. I am plain and grey,
painted by a human artist.
She respects my beauty, all silent and real.

I am drifting in heavens, amongst miles of clouds.
I am at peace now forever grey and beautiful,
just for a minute of eternity. To be what I am, conscious
of Life's gifts coursing within.

The sun, the stars, the wind, the land, the sea,
the men, the women, and the children – I understand all.
Now, I change to rain, so that all can live
and then I become all.

Fog

My love. I impugn the rules,
ruin our chance to rejoice,
here, in this house of rose-red flowers
You are a million bouquets.

And can I only cry – a gentle whimpering
of soul? Your ululation rises out.
All night it fogged.
We have carried many crosses.

I'm sorry that I over-depended on you.
Friend, I would lose you in this house
of tears, because of this canon,
surely, all love must be lost.

But my best falls short.
All is surely changed.
My Loyalty and my Betrayal has
separated me from You.

High above she wades through fog
below the fog-line
I step on sepia soil
and signal senseless semaphores.

The fog of love falls,
lifts to protect.
You tumble in a million shadows,
petals from a sky of violet light.

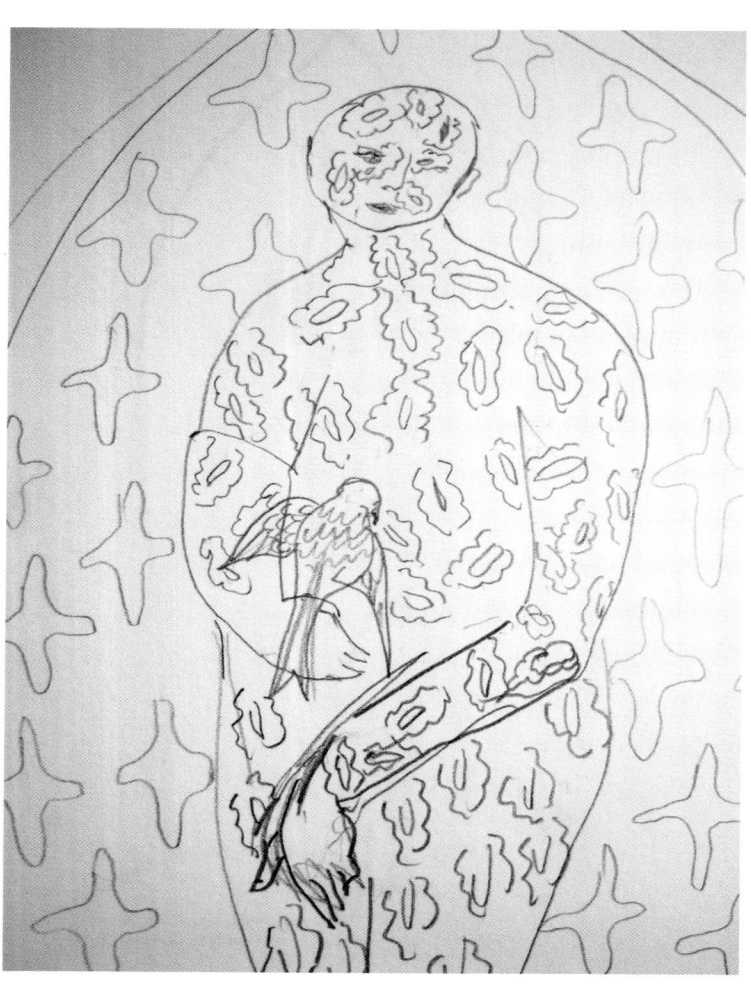

Beautiful World

Thou are a beautiful world.
I think of thee, sometimes
    night and day . . .

I ascend the sacred mountain.
and listen to the silent sound
    of the sea.

Prayers murmur down the mountain.
The cloud of tears opens.
    Tears fall all day.

A pair of ravens glides free.
Thou are a beautiful world.
  You and many others soar free.

Fenit Pier

Dedicated to Professor Tom Walsh, Mr. Tom McCormack, Professor Paul Redmond and Professor George Shorten (and their teams) for their care delivered over long hours and their understanding of *Man's Search for Meaning* by V. Frankl

A robust middle-aged man,
tweed jacket and glasses,
casts a drunken line,
leg lifted up
and holds on to flinging rod,
choreiform
dances and gyrates on Fenit pier.

Another man, long-haired,
green combat jacket
with three rods
works three lines.

Another with white jacket
and matching khaki trousers
tanned
fires the mepps
in a graceful lithe style
lands the perfect cast
and mullet.

The sturdy middle-aged man with the jerking
movements, some way or other,
holds on to the pier.
Going round and round
and everyone knows that he is a hero
against all odds.

Chorea describes involuntary and purposeless body movements occurring in diseases of the central nervous system

Ráiseanna na mBád 2009

Nuair a d'eitil an féileacán ó bhéilín Mhicilín
agus thaistil trí mhóinéir isteach trí chnámhshúil
an chapaill mhairbh is d'fhill arís ar ghob Mhicilín

bhog na naomhóga ar nós ciaróga dubha trasna bhéal an chuain.
. . . Bhí Fionntrá dubh le daoine . . . an domhan is a mháthair
ar cuairt ar ráiseanna Cheanntrá . . . ina measc Fear na bhFáinní.

Bhí Aogán Ó Rathaille ar theanga Mhuiris fós.
Bhí fear na gcártaí ann lena sheifteanna. D'ól Muiris
agus Tomás pórtar a chuirfeadh speabraídí ar aon duine.

Bhí foireann fear ón gCuas gléasta i ngeansaithe gorma
fir ó Bhailemhór gléasta i ngeansaithe bána
fir ón Leitriúch gléasta i ngeansaithe dearga
foireann ó Bhaile nGall gléasta i ngeansaithe dubha.

Ar an lá bhí an bua ag an gCuas
Up Cuas . . . an bád is tapúla
agus b'é Tadhg Dhiarmada bláth na bhfear.

Bhí caismirt idir Tomás – Bolcán Rí na Fraince –
agus fear tanaí na *Rings* – Dáire Donn Rí an domhain –
ar an ngaineamh. Bhí An tSrúill ag brúchtadh aníos
nuair a chaith Oscar an t-eachtrannach ar an dtrá . . .

D'fhág Muiris an t-Oileán nuair a bhí an Rí eile,
Rí an Oileáin, Seán Ó Catháin, ag bailiú na litreacha.
Anseo linn um thráthnóna ag Ráiseanna Cheanntrá. "Tar éis an triú
seans," a deir fear na gcártaí. Go mbeirimid beo ar an am seo arís.

Ghost Trawler

I observed a ghost trawler
anchor in the bay
under The Plough and The Milky Way.

The luminous lights shone round
and the ghost trawler
called me away, Northbound . . .

But my loved ones cannot come
with me now by the sweep of
light on Kerry Head sound.

The ghost trawler's lights shine round.
God forgive me for losing love throughout Time.
God forgive me for love that I've found.

The ghost trawler will call us by and by
when our Lives are complete,
then we shall all together be sea-bound . . .

Manuela Riedo R.I.P.

We see your radiant smile above The Corrib.
"Long have you waited for this journey to Ireland"
and two days later a horrible devastation struck you brutally
on the wasteland by Lough Atalia
as you walked from the Tiernan home in Renmore.

Are you no more? Hans and Arlette have lost their jewel.
You return in a casket to Hinterkappelen by Berne.
Forty-three students accompany your spirit home from Galway
of the welcomes – a town that has lost her innocence.

We are embarrassed and ashamed and we feel no end to this deep grief.
We are all diminished and betrayed as a race. The story makes a mockery
of our so called 5,000 years of Celtic civilisation.
We truly are more evil and less remorseful than Raskolnikov.

Manuela Riedo, our daughter, you shall rest
and we should rise up a monument
in witness to your lonely suffering and heinous homicide
on this wasteland. "*Yo la quise*".

We pray all months long with tears that your soul be released
and made glorious again and ascend with the swans
above the Corrib to your home in Hinterkappelen. The angels
come to your aid in Wohlen and Fribourg. "*Alleluia.*" "*Alleluia.*"

Have we not realized?

The Brent geese are returned again
to my favourite strand
where I shall meet you sometime –

Tralee to the right,
Kerry Head to the left,
and Fenit opposite.

I turn round – now, my back to the sea,
facing me – Sliabh Mis, Cathairconrí,
and dark Araglen.
I love you all so deeply.

A young farmer spreads fertiliser with his tractor.
I think of our families on this golden October evening
and wonder – have we not realized
that everyone would love each other ?

Cocaine

Big Bang poor boy high on cocaine
Crack shot six short salvoes
from close range to her brain.

Hedonists what have we to lose or gain
to pursue solipsism to the inane endgame?
Jekyll and Hyde in Heaven and Hell on coca-ethylene?

Lost his head stalking her through the twisting lane
and in his psychotic storm showed no pity but shame
what inglorious vice she endured and was slain.

Selling and buying the Incas' Snowbird, flying?
Homicide and Suicide – an epidemic of dying
the jasper country is shot by cocaine and crying.

22 year old beautician, Clare Bernal, was murdered by jilted boyfriend, Michael Pech, while he was high on cocaine.

The Radiant World
De Schone Wereld

by Albert Verwey (1865–1937)
(a version in translation from the original in Dutch)

For Peter and Máire

After a night's sleep I wake up
to a new creation on this beautiful day.

Everyday I gave, I give and I shall give
my life away (to You).

A day of my life shorter I see our radiant world
less selfishly, more lucent than ever.

Our world will be kinder when I depart
when the borders of our hearts are melted.

An Domhan Gleoite
A haithle **De Schone Wereld**

le Albert Verwey (1865–1937)
(aistriúchain ón Ollainis)

do Ruth and Lorcán

Gach maidin tar éis oíche suain cruthaítear
domhan úr dom ar an maidin breá seo

Gach lá thugas, tugaim, tabharfad
mo shaol (Duitse).

Lá eile caite as mo shaol (cónaítheoir gearrshaolach), áfach,
chím an domhan gleoite níos neamhleithleasaí, níos niamhraí dá réir.

Beidh ár ndomhan lách níos soilsí nuair a fhágfaidh mé,
nuair a leáfaidh teorainneacha ár n-anam ina chéile.

Mary Magdalene, only Time will tell

The seven oarsmen row us in a golden boat
to this shore of tears,
my favourite of all places, but I am insecure
because of my love and fears.

Thou and I create a single energy
as we might live in harmony with
the spirit of life in a freefall synergy.

Who would have dreamt life so dual?
We face Death and Life fearsomely and
are under both human and divine rule.

But how is it that truly I fell
though in fear of Christ and Mananán Mac Lir?
Mary Magdalene, only Time will tell.

Thomas Hardy

(For Nóirín, Rachel, Ruth and Peter)

When I fingered through a brown folder of poetry rejection slips recently
which I then destroyed, I recalled how the great Hardy must have felt
– anxious and dejected when rejected by Alexander MacMillan.

Tom, a student of Architecture, sketched the house at Bockhampton,
so wild with snakes, bats and heathcropper
and portrayed Emma under the waterfall. "Fair beloved, our bed is green…"

Dorchester close by . . . just a stone's throw.
Well he knew about the Mayor of Casterbridge – Michael Henchard
was a troubled soul and so his daughter, Elizabeth-Jane.

But Stonehenge awaited his sacrificial heroine.
Tom said, "I've never put it on paper . . . what she was or is to me."
Tom, you surely tried in the 508 page *oeuvre*

I read of that tumultuous emotional experience.
It may all have started as a sort of joke – when the parson called
"plain Jack Durbeyfield" "Sir John from the lineage of D'Urbervilles".

Angel Clare felt a passion for the natural,
soft and silent Tess and abandoned her when
he learned that she had been defiled.

She murdered her rapist, Alec D'Urbervilles.
"Outside the inexorable," said Tess. "Within was affection, union,
error forgiven" while Tess slept with Angel Clare, finally at peace.

Were you Emma or some other blue-eyed Pharmakos
to be slain for the sins of pagan mankind?
Tom sacrificed our tragic heroine, Tess, to the sun at Stonehenge.

Emma and Tom yearned for reconciliation . . . a second attempt . . .
only to be expected . . . a normal event for us all
after thirty years of childless marriage . . . Emma you presented him
with a Bible at the end of a millennium. Emma and Tom visited Éire.

Yeats rewarded him with a medal. Tom, you fell in love with Florence
    Henniker –
hook, line and sinker . . .her terracotta dress looked drizzly and dazzling in
    the rain . . .
you and she were soul-mates . . .
but another Florence – Dugdale – became the second wife

after Emma died in 1912. Tom – he loved you, Emma, more than ever.
The Titanic floundered. He turned to poems as "the darkling thrush do sing"
    and I
returned to my failed fiction when we acknowledged our Departures.

Thomas Hardy II
Thomas and Emma Hardy

Emma and Tom cycled
the quiet roads of Dorset

Tom on his "Rover Cob"
Emma on her green bike, "The grasshopper".

They toured forty miles
a day near Dorchester.

Returning from a harvest festival in Tunworth,
they pedalled together under the moonlight
    for seventeen miles.

Tom biked it to Southampton
– fifty miles there and back
to see the troops embarking for South Africa.

Later Emma rode a blue bicycle
dressed in her blue cycling suit,
housed her bicycle in the bicycle room
    at Max Gate.

Together, Emma and Tom, toured
the quiet roads of Dorset early and late.

Thomas Hardy III

Bath

In Bath, Tom loved Emma
and would walk the world with her.

He thought about Bathsheba Everdene
when she rode high on her saddle.

He was Gabriel Oaks and would always
be there for his Emma.

Gabriel Oaks was always strong, a safe pair of hands.
Bathsheba did not want to be thought men's property

and when Sgt Troy mesmerised her at first
and then stole away . . . Gabriel picked up the pieces.

Gabriel was there for Bathsheba . . . a natural union.
Emma moved from their nuptial bed to the attic overhead.

Emma expired in 1912.
And he loved you, Emma, more than ever.

Thomas Hardy IV
Wessex

Florence Dugdale lived with Tom
after Emma's death.

Her dog, Wessex, a biter,
was feared by everyone.

Tom was sixty-five and Florence was twenty-six
thirty-nine years life between them.

Florence became the second wife and served him
home-made cakes, thin bread and butter.

Thomas Hardy V
Troy

Leslie Stephen, Virginia Woolf's father
owned a dog named Troy.

He was no biter
like Wessex.

Leslie edited the *Cornhill*
and serialised – *Far From The Madding Crowd.*

He worried about Sgt. Troy, the philanderer,
and Bathsheba causing a scandal.

So it did and Henry James lambasted
not Troy, nor Sgt. Troy but Thomas Hardy.

Thomas Hardy VI
Virginia Woolf

Virginia thanked Tom for the sonnet that he
dedicated to her father, Leslie.

Tom was human, aware that perceived shame and rejection
required divine healing.
He must think of his friend, Horace Moule, who died
by suicide . . . "Easy to die . . . love to my mother."

Humble Virginia, another poet-novelist,
loved Tom's poetry and Mrs Dalloway.

Thomas Hardy VII
Death

"Grow old
along with me.

Give me kettle broth,
grilled bacon
and some grapes.

I never let a day go by
without using a pen."

The wizard concealed his magic
behind an ordinariness.

His heart placed in a casket to Stinsford churchyard.
His ashes placed in an urn in Poets' Corner at Westminster Abbey
to the backdrop of Handel's *Dead March* from *Saul*.

The end?
Hardly.

St. Molaga, pray for us

I give you my love that was
built by day and fell by night.
St. Molaga, pray for us.

Guide us to your abbey
that we rebuild
with envy, doubt and despair.
St. Molaga, pray for us.

I light my candle on a sheaf of corn.
Let it float to you, my love,
on the river Argideen.
St. Molaga, pray for us.

Let the candle-light of Timoleague
sanctify us – *Kyrie. Gloria. Sanctus.*
Alleluia. Alleluia. Alleluia.
St. Molaga, pray for us.

NOTE: *St. Molaga attempted many times to build his abbey but failed . . . where he built was incorrect . . . What he had built by day fell by night. He dreamed if he placed a candle stick on a sheaf of corn it would float to where the Abbey should be built in Timoleague, Co. Cork.*

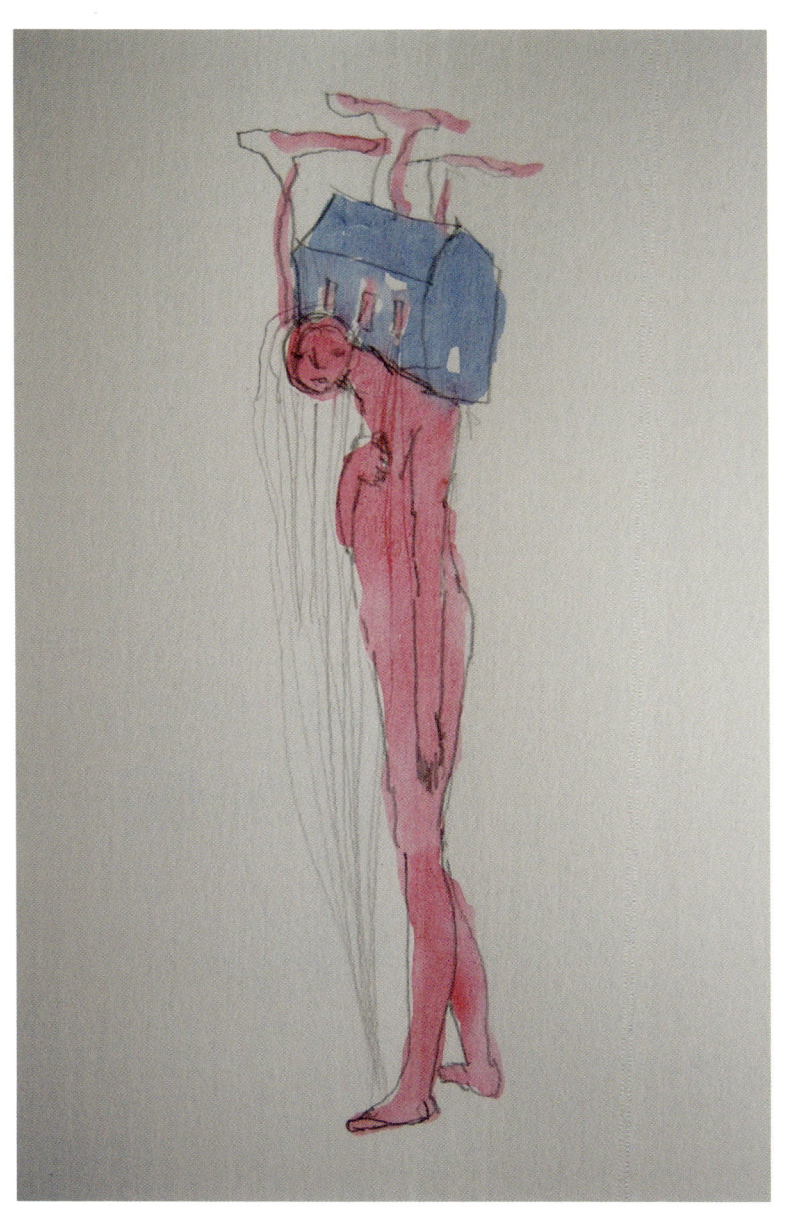

43

We are all Haitians

(For Jim and Áine, Fiach, Hannah, Muiris, Séamas, and Martha)

We are all Haitians.
The palace and the cathedral
have fallen.
It's appalling –
Archbishop Miot
thrown from his balcony is dead.
President René Préval cannot find a bed!
We are trapped here in the Necropolis,
City of the Dead.
Corpses piled in heaps at *Port au Prince* –
a disaster of Nature that makes no sense.

We are all Lesotheans,
Ethiopians,
Zimbabweans, Malawians,
and Haitians.

We are the world's poor.
We have contracted HIV
malaria and T.B.
Our children are malnourished –
as thin with marasmus
so swollen with kwashiorkor,
washed out by dysentery
left without encouragement.
We are all Haitians.

We have no self-confidence.
We are the unemployed.
We are conspired against.
We are the raped.
We have lost your respect.
We have lost everything.

We, the unloved,
we, the confused,
we, the unwanted
want to die.
We, the injured,
we have died a thousand times.
We are the very depressed
dying in solitude.

But we shall rebuild a safer Haiti.
We are all Haitians.

Publications

English Poetry:
THE LOVE LETTERS OF DANIEL O'CONNELL (Inné, Dúnchaoin,1992) and Institute of Public Administration for D.O.C.A.L. in PEOPLE POWER, (Dublin, 1993) edited by Maurice R. O'Connell, (pgs 112-127)
TOMBOLO (Lapwing Publications, Belfast, 1995)
VERBUM ET VERBUM (Salmon Publishing, 1997 and 1998)
THE SEPARATION OF GREY CLOUDS (Salmon Publishing, 2002)
HOMAGE (Salmon Publishing, 2006)
ECHOES AND SHADOWS (Robert Hale, London, 2008)

Filíocht Ghaeilge:
AN SOLAS GEAL LONRACH (Coiscéim, 1992)
DÉITHE AN tSOLAIS (Coiscéim,1994)
MISE A SHAOLAÍTEAR (Coiscéim, 1997)
Ó LÁ GO LÁ (Coiscéim, 2004)
BRIATHAR AND SOLAS (Coiscéim, 2008)

Translation:
GODDESSES AND GODS OF LIGHT (Lapwing, Belfast,1997)
PARNELL TO QUEENIE LE PÁDRAIG Ó SNODAIGH (Lapwing, Belfast, 2001)
THE WORD AND LIGHT (Somerville Press, 2008)